# DING DONG THE BELL PUSSY IN THE WELL

*Poems by Linda Lerner*

*Drawings by Donna Kerness*

©2014 Linda Lerner
©2014 Art by Donna Kerness

All rights reserved. No part of this book may be reproduced without the express written permission of the author, except in the case of written reviews.

ISBN 978-1-929878-51-2

First edition

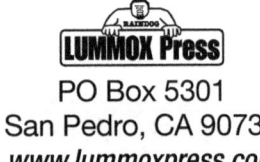

PO Box 5301
San Pedro, CA 90733
*www.lummoxpress.com*

Printed in the United States of America

**ACKNOWLEDGMENTS**

"Ring Around the Rosy" and "What Just Happened" appeared in *Danse Macabre*, 7/5/2013

"Jack's Road" appeared in *Gutter Eloquence*, #28, Oct. 2013

**A special thanks to Louis Walence for his computer/technical assistance**

**CONTENTS**

We  | 7

What Just Happened  | 9

Catch Me If You Can  | 11

The Sound of London Bridges Falling in NYC  | 13

Ring Around the Rosy: A Danse Macabre  | 15

The Mother Who Gives Birth to a Poem  | 17

Remember, remember the Fifth of November  | 19

Stumbling on Jack's Road  | 21

An Old Wives Tale or a Rip Van Winkle Story  | 23

When Every Color Became Red  | 25

Humpty Dumpty  | 27

Notes  | 28

Bios  | 29

[1]This rhyme dates back to the 13th century. During outbreaks of the Bubonic Plague strangers were looked upon with fear. Dogs barking alerted the townspeople to them.

> "Hark hark the dogs do bark
> The beggars are coming to town
> Some in rags and some in juags
> And one in a velvet gown."

## We

we are the wandering minstrels and troubadours
the same who went from city to town eight centuries ago
disguised in current garb and language
we wander from café to bar to anywhere
we can be heard
hatching  plots against injustice in our songs of self
we are not the laureate prized ones
who pretend to be us….sometimes stand among us
we are the poorly paid part time jobless ones
no one takes seriously…
*hark hark the dogs do bark*
echo in the air when we cross accepted lines
it's the bark of disapproval in people's eyes
that spurs us on even more
we are the ones often mistaken for beggars
who've marched, protested on lines
running off the page to camp out
on the muddy earth for days to free the earth
for those who heckle and fear us as though
we are bringing the plague to them
which of course we are

[1] "Ding Dong Bell" is a phrase Shakespeare used in several plays. In the original lyrics the cat was left to drown.

**"The Tempest, Act I, Scene II:**
"Sea nymphs hourly ring his knell:
Hark! Now I hear them - Ding, dong, bell."

**The Merchant of Venice, Act III, Scene II:**"Let us all ring fancy's bell; I'll begin it - Ding, dong, bell."

Ding dong bell
Pussy's in the well
Who put her in?
Little Johnny Flynn
Who pulled her out?
Little Tommy Stout
What a naughty boy was that
Try to drown poor Pussycat,
Who ne'er did any harm
But killed all the mice
In the Farmer's barn!

## What Just Happened?

a woman opens her bag on a crowded subway
takes out a mirror and asks the stranger
seated next to her to hold it up; she reaches into her purse for
black eyeliner and begins to haul up a cat from somewhere
deep inside....
        ding dong the bell
        pussy in the well
        who put her there

This middle aged man doesn't know what is happening
 but something....he's been taking the same train every morning
and nothing like this has ever
others try to ignore what they see
look down uneasily at their cell phones when the train
stalls  the lights go out and everyone disappears as though
sucked into a great hole...
        ding dong the bell
        people in the well
        who put them there
the man feels this cat eyed being nestled against his mind
quickly crossing boundaries
his briefcase lies on his lap forgotten when
suddenly the lights come on and
the train starts to move taking her with it;

the man looks around, bewildered, rubs his eyes and
stands up; he must have dozed off for a few minutes
others looks up from I Pads, books, papers, from somewhere else
they've never been to see where they are
and how much further they must travel

## Catch Me If You Can

¹This is a cat and bird story full of trees and walls
of climbing up one and jumping over the other

*Up went pussy cat and down went he;*
*Down came pussy, and away Robin ran*

I watched his eyes scamper up one
after me while we sat in a café drinking coffee
then making love thru the park, ignoring
the temptation trees posed till next morning's
clawing disagreement set human & animal off
in a shift shaping chase....

*Says little robin red breast,*
    *'catch me if you can'*

this is about a bird flying in and out of a cat's sight
trying  to elude him while praying catch me

this is about the life two people led;
I listen for his sound, for what would send
my heart flying up to the highest branch
and when I'd gotten comfortable thought
he was gone, I was safe, he'd spring out
and I'd jump...Sometimes I felt like the cat
chasing myself and he was the bird
sometimes the other way around

and so it went    and then it didn't

[1]The first London Bridge was made of wood and clay during the Roman occupation of England and was fortified or re-built with the various materials. "Many disasters struck the bridges - Viking invaders destroyed the bridge in the 1000's which led to a fortified design, complete with a drawbridge. Building materials changed due to the many fires that broke out on the bridge."

## The Sound of London Bridges Falling in NYC

it's London bridges falling into familiar song in my head
as I stare at the bridge linking Brooklyn to Manhattan
being repaired: a white cloth flung over it
conceals small cracks, fractures
what's not yet visible in my bones

      bridge that links who I am to who I was
      falling down, falling down

*build it up with wood and clay*, but
wood and clay wash away like worn out words
side effects of shoddy workmanship, the latest drugs:
bridges suddenly snap

a bridge can only be poemed so many times
before it gives, won't le me cross over
to then and them and who I was

*build it up with bricks and mortar*
but they won't stay; I retouch photos with
white lies that no longer work when
life isn't digital

*build it up with iron and steel* determination
but iron and steel start to bend and bow
beneath the weight of facts


And as for *silver and gold*
they'll *be stolen away* by those who
offer placebo promises they market for a price
                      and
won't shut out the sound of London bridges falling down
bridges falling   falling

## Ring Around the Rosy: A Danse Macabre

[1]The nursery rhyme dates back to the Bubonic plague of London in 1661 when a rosy rash in the shape of a ring appeared on the skin. People believed that the disease was transmitted by bad smells, so they filled pockets with sweet smelling herbs or posies. Ashes refer to the cremation of dead bodies.

the rash is unseen, isn't a rash but
for the sake of this nursery rhyme
for the game you're playing
around what turned your office upside down spinning
around the fear something is wrong and
spread like a rash when you scratched it

began playing *ring around the rosy*
*A pocket full of poses* of magical thinking
to snuff out the smell of ashes from
cigarettes you stopped smoking,
lengthening your life line with more and
more tasks around a skipped heartbeat chased
around hours of waiting for test results
around everyone you know running around
what you can't see or smell around what
you feel in your gut:
game played in childhood innocence--
*We all fall down*

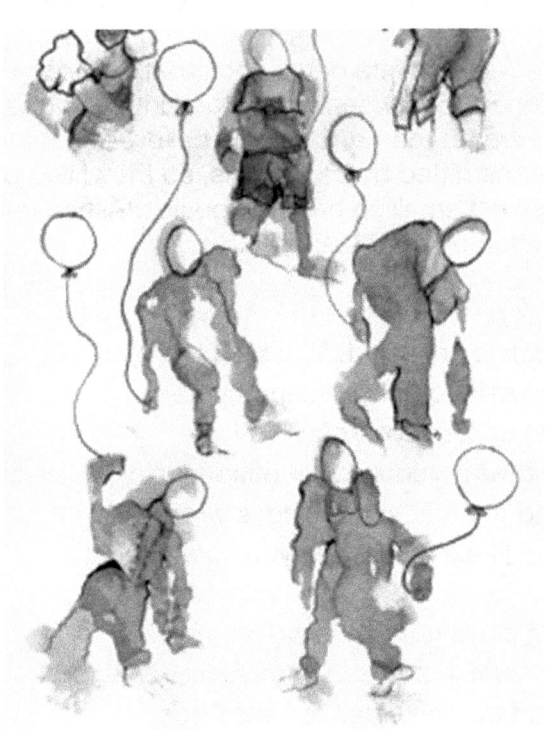

[1]Mondays child is fair of face,
Tuesdays child is full of grace,
Wednesdays child is full of woe,
Thursdays child has far to go,
Fridays child is loving and giving,
Saturdays child works hard for his living,
And the child that is born on the Sabbath day
Is bonny and blithe, and good and gay.

## The Mother Who Gives Birth to a Poem

it was like that mother goose rhyme without the rhyme sense of it,
you know how it goes, Monday's child is fair of face
                              Tuesday's child is....
only he wasn't a child or fair and it wasn't that simple....
seven days  seven images  a mother wasn't needed for
nobody's newborn middle aged child of the 21$^{st}$ century
to give birth to himself in this new world
send out an announcement of that day's birth...

they say Wednesday's child is full of woe, and
there were days he didn't understand why nobody
commented more on his new birth, didn't they see
the cool cat playing the sax the activist on stage
working the crowd, the lover women flock over
seen the birth announcements coming daily
more & more rapidly especially on weekends...

she says Saturdays child works hard for its living
and it was hard work to keep it up
he thought about his Russian grandmother who had eight children
pioneer women out west who died giving birth
people spoke of a woman's first, second, and third families...
now a man could know what it feels like too...sort of...
he left his apartment less and less, the days of the week
kept repeating and he was always back to Monday,
another due date...

others were too busy with their own births to give
him more than a cursory acknowledgment
the announcements piled up, un read, unlooked at
as if he'd died; posthumous births kept coming;
they kept coming and coming....

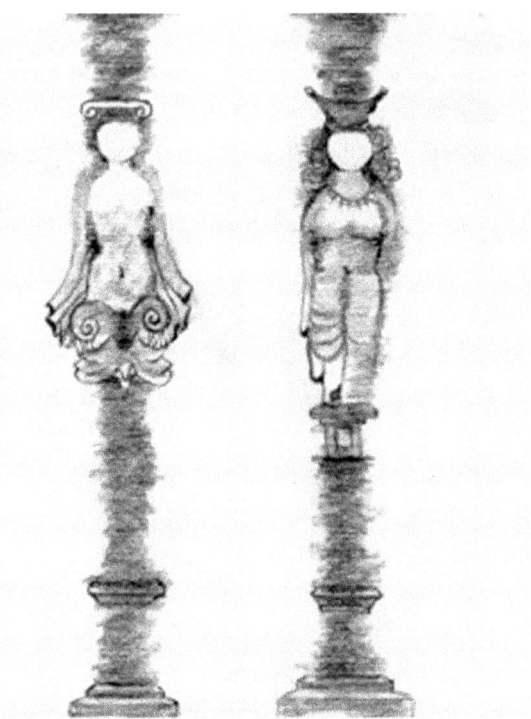

[1]On the 5th November 1605 Guy Fawkes was caught in the cellars of the Houses of Parliament with several dozen barrels of gunpowder. Guy Fawkes was subsequently tried as a traitor with his co-conspirators for plotting against the government.

> *"Remember remember the fifth of November*
> *Gunpowder, treason and plot.*
> *I see no reason why gunpowder, treason*
> *Should ever be forgot... "*

**Remember remember the Fifth of November**

yes, even that…what happened centuries ago
points to what I can't forget and am afraid
will vanish into oblivion, two 70 foot columns
all that will remain of what happened that day

fail to become a lightening strike against
facts twisted out of shape like that steel beam
salvaged from the wreckage

and even that isn't always enough
to bring back what it felt like

"I see no reason why gunpowder, treason
        should ever be forgot…." they sang in 1605

remember   remember   March 25
the triangle shirtwaist factory fire my mother often spoke of
came back to me  on May 17th
like a thread pulled through decades and
yanked out of  Banglasdesh in New York City

remember  remember…
the first betrayal…first act of treason

forget nothing….

[1]The reference is to Black Jack, an English pirate who was famous for escaping from the authorities in the late 16th century hence Jack be nimble...

> *Jack be nimble*
> *Jack be quick*
> *Jack jump over*
> *The candlestick.*

## Stumbling on Jack's Road

*Jack be nimble Jack be quick*
Jack jumped over all the Johns who
couldn't imagine their way past ordinary
walked between lines they never crossed
*I'm Jack* he said, furious if anyone forgot,
a name which summoned up those who've imprinted
their souls on a nation's myth:  the king of the beats
two dare devil SF poets*, a president   a fighter
at night when his brain speeded so he couldn't sleep
he conjured up the notorious: Jack Legs Diamond
a 16$^{th}$ century pirate called Black Jack…
known as a jack of all trades, he composed, wrote, painted
fast as he could:
    *Jack be nimble Jack be quick*
    Jack flew into the sky
crashing into middle age, broke
this wasn't supposed to happen, not to a Jack…
he rose up out of a jumble or words
spewed out on paper nobody understood
debt ridden as the country…owed his whole life
to his name that came up empty
a woman needy enough would make him
her child, bring him back to what he was
going to be, back to his namesake
the kind of man I could fall in love with
*I'm Jack*, he said when we met
only I knew better.


*The reference is to Jack Micheline and Jack Hirschman

[1]This isn't technically a mother goose nursery rhyme, but a superstition that dates back to about 1905. Many variations, like the following, have been written along this line:

> Step on a line, break your mother's spine
> Step on a hole, break your mother's sugar bowl
> Step on a nail, you'll put your dad in jail

**An Old Wives Tale or A Rip Van Winkle Story**

"step on a crack, you'll break your mother's back"
nothing about stepping over it, landing on the other side
stooped over in pain, the weight of seven decades presses down on you;
"step on a line, you'll break your mother's spine"
she's long dead  it's your spine, came down
a curved genetic road to find you
the man of the house after your father left;

cracks formed, the fine line between decisions
stepped over without consequences widened as
you walked the same pedestrian route habit mapped:
easiest distance between  years:  from home to work to the
same restaurant you and your mother once frequented

a struggle now to stand upright, you fight against
the downward gravitational pull of seventy years;
I do what I can, errands, simple tasks; not enough
the doctor gives you shots; it take away the pain

you go back to who you were
and can never be again...

who's that old woman in the picture, my mother once asked
when I showed her a photo I took of her one day...
who's that man  hunched over a cane I once couldn't
keep up with he walked so fast, who's that angry man
raging against injustice who reminds me of my father
....what happened to the one I've been leaning on all these years?

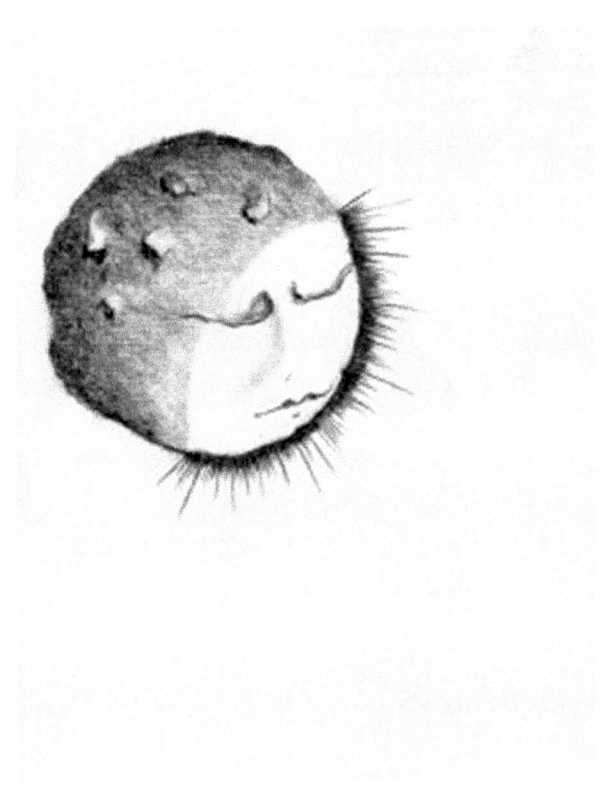

**When Every Color Became Red**

> [1] *"Red sky at night*
> *Sailors' delight;*
> *Red sky at morning,*
> *sailors take warning"*

no sailor but he can predict weather
interpret the signs as well as any of them
doesn't need to hear doctors' forecasts
tell him what he forgets when he closes
his eyes at night and all the red inside his head
burning red rage is turned out and
he can see as well as he ever did before....

it's different in the morning
his fear barely contained when
he wakes bumps into a table and
strikes out blindly, his nerves like match sticks ....
can't see the face of his closest friend approaching
misses a step and red spills out of him
coloring his sky, every color of his life burning
red as all hell, red as the pitch black
dark he's slowly being thrust into

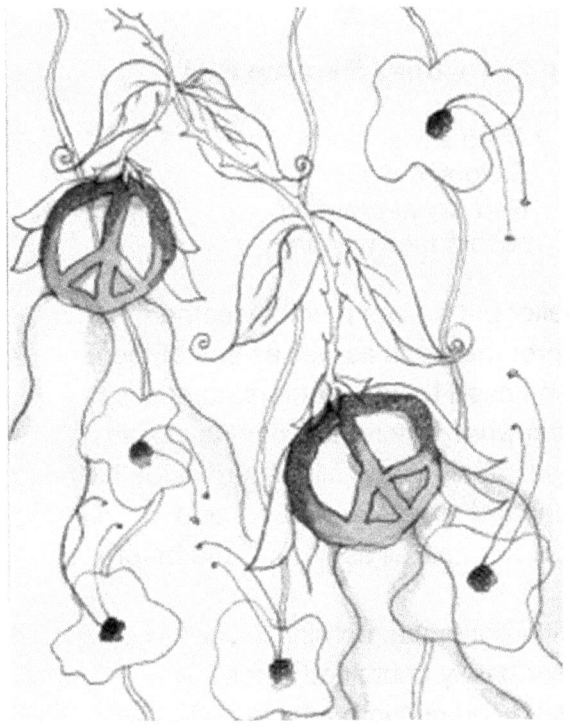

[1]Humpty Dumpty was believed to be a large cannon used during the English Civil War.(1642-1649) in the siege of Colchester. This was a walled town. Next to the city's wall was Saint Mary's church. A huge cannon was placed on the wall. It was fired on by "One-eyed Jack Thompson." The shot damaged the wall, which caused the cannon to fall. It was too heavy for anyone to put it together again

## Humpty Dumpty

a cannon called Humpty dumpty seated on
a centuries' old wall is set to go off....
you know him from the rhyme,
the big egg shaped androgynous one
glimpsed thru Alice's looking glass bragging
if he fell all the king's men and horses would come etc.

I am humpty dumpty
there are no kings men, no horses
hair line cracks of broken promises,
laws twisted out of shape aimed at this wall
I grew up on, painted live flowers over
and from it dangled peace signs like crosses
and the star of David: this wall
no one will fix is my birth rite

I am a generation
I have never lived anywhere else

kicked out of the womb and
thrust onto it  I looked down
and jumped without ever leaving the wall

jumped  again and again....fearless
the wall was my safety net, promises to insure it
were made insuring the dream of the wall

I was immortal on it; when
disease struck an army of drugs killed death
for a while...then aimed at me

I was positioned to fall off the wall
and be put back together  but
the wall is crumbling beneath me
into the old rhyme where all the kings men, etc.

when I fall a generation will fall with me
nobody will come to put us back together again

**All footnotes:**

[1]**Source**: *Nursery Rhymes Lyrics, Origins & History*
*www.rhymes.org.uk*

**Linda Lerner's** *Takes Guts & Years Sometimes* was published by *NYQ Books*, June, 2011; she's previously published thirteen collections of poetry and been nominated twice for a pushcart prize. Her poems have recently been in New *Verse News, Gutter Eloquence, The Brooklyn Voice, Danse Macabre, Two Bridges, Presa, Fall, 2011* (featured poet*) Lummox, Home Planet News, Big Hammer*, and *The Mom Egg*; her essay *"Land Grab: Putting Down Stakes"* appeared in *The Brooklyn Voice*, March, 2013. Her next collection, *Yes, the Ducks Were Real*, will be published by *NYQ Books*.

**Donna Kerness** has been producing Art of various mediums over the years. Her inspirations have emerged from her past... She was a Dancer at the Henry Street Playhouse with Alwin Nikolais, and Murray Louis, a casual fellow poet and friend of Linda Lerner, and an Underground Cinema Super Star, in the movies of the Kuchar Brothers, during the Sixties in New York.

After relocating to San Antonio and raising a family, now is working with Sketching, Drawing, Painting and Multimedia Art which has been exhibited at the Highwire Gallery, in San Antonio, Texas.

The LUMMOX Press publishes chapbooks, the Little Red Book series, perfect bound books (the Respect series), a poetry anthology (yearly) and e-books. The stated goal of the press is to elevate the bar for poetry, while bringing the 'word' to an international audience. We are proud to offer this chapbook as part of that effort.

For more information and to see our growing catalog of choices, please go to *www.lummoxpress.com/lc*

www.ingramcontent.com/pod-product-compliance
Lightning Source LLC
Chambersburg PA
CBHW060622070426
42449CB00042B/2467